How to Handle Your SCHOOL

By Roy Apps

Illustrated by Jo Moore

EDGE
FRANKLIN WATTS

LONDON·SYDNEY

This edition first published in 2014
by Franklin Watts

Text © Roy Apps 2014
Interior illustrations © Jo Moore 2014
Cover illustration © Nick Sharratt 2014
Cover design by Cathryn Gilbert
Layouts by Blue Paw Design

Franklin Watts
338 Euston Road
London NW1 3BH

Franklin Watts Australia
Level 17/207 Kent Street
Sydney, NSW 2000

A CIP catalogue record for this book
is available from the British Library.

(pb) ISBN: 978 1 4451 2394 3
(ebook) ISBN: 978 1 4451 2398 1
(Library ebook) ISBN: 978 1 4451 2402 5

1 3 5 7 9 10 8 6 4 2

Printed in Great Britain

Franklin Watts is a division of Hachette Children's Books,
an Hachette UK company.
www.hachette.co.uk

How to Handle Your SCHOOL

By Roy Apps

Illustrated by Jo Moore

Contents

It was a dark and stormy night............ 6

SAS Handling Skills Training 1:
Teachers..................................... 17

Quiz 1: What Kind Of Super-Teacher
Have You Got?.............................. 22

Quiz 2: Why Has Your Teacher Taken
A Job That Involves Spending All Day
With You Lot?.............................. 26

Quiz 3: Dummies Guide To Super-
Teacher Engineering........................ 31

Quiz 4: How To Neutralise Your Super-
Teachers' Weapons.......................... 40

Quiz 5: On The Use Of Neutralising
Agents..................................... 50

SAS Handling Skills Training 2:
Friends And Enemies........................ 52

Quiz 6: How To Work Out What Type Of Super-Enemies You Have Got.......... 55

Quiz 7: Handling Super-Enemies........ 59

Quiz 8: How To Work Out What Type Of Super-Friends You Have Got............... 63

Quiz 9: Finding Out What Super-Friends And Super-Enemies Are Made Of.......... 71

SAS Handling Skills Training 3: Headteachers................................. 75

Quiz 10: Hunt The Headteacher......... 80

SAS Handling Skills Training 4: The Man Of Mystery........................ 84

Quiz 11: Cool It Anger...................... 86

Quiz 12: The Battle Of The Scaretaker   90

How this book starts...

It was a dark and stormy night and I was snuggled up in bed dreaming pleasant dreams about all the kind and useful things I'd done with my life, like squirting shaving foam into the teachers' coffee machine and watching them all rush into lessons foaming at the mouth when...

CRASH!!!
bang!
MEEEUUUUUUW!

I leapt up with a start and found myself staring into two large wild menacing eyes.

Quickly, I wrestled my teddy bear onto the floor, got out of bed and decided to go and get myself a glass of milk.

On the way I noticed two things:

1. The front door was open.

And…

2. There was a double trail of two sets of muddy footprints leading down the hall to the kitchen.

I knew this could mean one of only two things:

Tiddles, my cat, had given up on using the cat flap and had opened the front door with a set of keys, wearing two pairs of my boots.

Or…

I'd got burglars!

I followed the footprints to the kitchen. They stopped at the fridge door. Ah, now I knew the truth!

Tiddles had wanted some milk! I pulled open the fridge door. Tiddles leapt out, disguised as two girls wearing superhero masks and carrying pink and blue **Megapower Water Blasters**.

"Freeze!" yelled one of the masked maidens.

Well, I'm not stupid. I knew what to do.

Straightaway, I leapt into the fridge's ice-cube compartment. Then a thought struck me.

It's cold in here!!!

Then I thought, get out there and stand up for yourself. So I did.

"Don't shoot. What do you want?" I asked.

"Are you the World's Number One Handling Expert?" asked one girl.

I nodded. "You bet. I've written books on how to handle teachers, mums, dads..."

"OK, OK," said the other girl, "we don't want your life story. We're here because we need your help."

"My help," I frowned. "Mmmm, now where did I leave it? Oh yes, my help — it's in my wardrobe."

The two girls ran off. Ha! I'd got rid of them! It was so easy-peasy!

But they came back...

"Did you find my help?" I asked them.

"No," said one of the girls, "but we did find this." From behind her back she produced my teddy and put her **Megapower Water Blaster** to his head.

"You're going to help us or the teddy gets it," said the other girl.

"OK, OK, I'll help you," I said. "But for goodness sake, don't hurt my teddy. I couldn't bear it."

"Aaargh," groaned one of the girls. "They warned us your jokes would be bad."

I was bundled into the back of an unmarked van. Well, it was unmarked when we left, but by the time we stopped it was very marked indeed — mainly with impressions of my face on the window where I had been bounced around.

Eventually, the van screeched to a halt, the back doors opened and I was bundled out. I knew this could mean only one thing: we'd arrived!

Stretching out before us was a vast jungle. Exotic birds screeched in the trees and the air was hot and humid. A group of children ran to join us.

I looked up and saw a sign above my head which read:

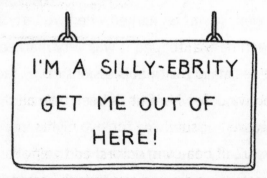

I'M A SILLY-EBRITY GET ME OUT OF HERE!

"Shouldn't that say '*I'm a Celebrity... Get Me Out Of Here!*'?" I asked.

The girl with the pink *Megapower Water Blasters* took off her mask and said:

> No, it shouldn't.
> Let me introduce myself.
> My name's Maz.

Then the girl with the blue blaster took off her mask.

> That's right, her name's Maz and these two lads are our mates, Chas and Naz. I'm Daniella-Marie.

Then Naz said:

"We've set up this special kids' *I'm a Celebrity... Get Me Out Of Here!* We all did really well at surviving for two nights in a tank full of boa constrictors, and going for an early morning dip in our wonderful crocodile-infested lake, but there was one test that turned all four of us into jabbering wrecks."

Maz, Chas, Naz and Daniella-Marie took me past the lake over to a large hut. Above the door was a sign.

"That sign fills me with gloom and foreboding," I said.

"It fills me with worse than foreboding," said Maz. "It fills me with fiveboding."

The sign read:

Then I swung the sign round the right way and it read:

SCHOOL

"Two things are obvious," I explained. "One, unless somebody is playing a really nasty joke, that hut is a school. And two — this is an entirely new type of school, where the staff and pupils are more resistant to my usual handling skills."

"What can we do?" asked Chas.

"There is only one thing for it. You must all go back to school with me to do some SAS training."

"Hey, cool! Does that mean we get to train with the army?" asked Naz, excitedly.

"No, not that kind of SAS training," I explained. "This kind of SAS training is a lot tougher and scarier than the army's SAS training. This SAS training is Super Advanced School Handling Skills Training. Well, are you up for it?"

Maz, Chas, Naz and Daniella-Marie looked uncertain.

"You'll learn how to handle school," I said.

Maz, Chas, Naz and Daniella-Marie still looked uncertain.

"You'll get your very own How To Handle School Advanced Handler's Badge," I went on.

"Yeah! Cool! We're up for it!" yelled Maz, Chas, Naz and Daniella-Marie.

"Then let's go," I said.

"Where to?" asked Maz, Chas, Naz and Daniella-Marie.

"To the next page, of course," I replied.

SAS Handling Skills Training 1

Teachers

So the next day, at a quarter to nine, I met Maz, Chas, Naz and Daniella-Marie round the back of their school — Downwith School.

"Let's go in the front," moaned Maz.

"We don't want to attract attention," I said.

"Why would we do that?" asked Maz.

"Well, you're wearing an army jacket and carrying a **Megapower Water Blaster**," I replied. "That's why I'm wearing the Downwith School uniform under my normal clothes. Look..."

Argh!

"You're wearing
the Downwith School girls'
uniform," pointed out
Daniella-Marie.

"Oh you're SOOOOOO
picky," I complained.

Half an hour later I came back wearing
the boys' uniform.

"There, is that any better?" I asked.

"Not really," said Maz.

"Look," I said, crossly,
"are we here to learn
Super Advanced
School Handling
Skills or are we here
to film an edition of
Gok Wan's latest
fashion series?"

"OK," said Maz.

"OK," said Naz.

"OK," said Daniella-Marie.

"KO," said Chas, whose spelling wasn't really up to much.

"Now the first rule of SAS handling is that not all teachers are the same," I began.

"Shouldn't you tell us your name?" asked Daniella-Marie.

I stared at all four of them, straight between the eyes. "They call me," I said, "the Quizmister. Now let's get on with your Super Advanced School Handling Skills training. The first rule is—"

"What kind of a name's that?" interrupted Chas.

"It's the sort of name for a mister who sets quizzes," I said. "Satisfied?"

Chas frowned. "Not really," he said. "I mean it's not a proper name, is it—"

"Sit down," I told Maz, Naz and Daniella-Marie. So, they did. Right on top of Chas.

At last I could continue. I said again, this time in capital letters.

"REMEMBER! NOT ALL TEACHERS ARE THE SAME."

"I've never thought about it before," said Naz, "but you're right. Like Mr Stubble has a beard, but Miss Tache hasn't."

"No," agreed Maz, "she's got a moustache."

← **Mr Stubble**

Miss Tache →

"There you are then," I said. "So the first SAS Handling Skill you have to learn is how to recognise what sort of Super-Teacher you have. You can do this by working out what abilities your Super-Teacher has. All you need to do is complete..." (You have to turn over to find out.)

Quiz 1: What Kind Of Super-Teacher Have You Got?

These teachers have super abilities. Do any of them sound familiar? I bet they do. So, on a piece of paper, write down the numbers which apply to teachers at your school. (Answers on page 25.)

SUPER-TEACHER ABILITY 1

TEACHER'S NAME: Ms F. Errari

ABILITY: Super Speed

That's right, Ms F Errari is so fast, she makes Sebastian Vettel look like a tortoise with its shoelaces tied together.

So...

Does Ms F Errari use her Super Speed to:

1. Race round to the supermarket to buy a large tin of chocolate biscuits for your class?

2. Race to the school office halfway through your lesson and ring the bell for break so that you all get an extra half-an-hour playtime?

3. Race you and the rest of your class at such a speed during lessons that you have no energy left during break to do really useful stuff like kicking footballs onto the school kitchen roof.

SUPER-TEACHER ABILITY 2

TEACHER'S NAME:
Mr Adder
ABILITY: Maths wizard

That's right, Mr Adder is such a wizard at maths, he can do mental maths standing on his head. It's just a pity you can't do mental maths standing on his head.

So...

Does Mr Adder use his maths wizardry to:

1. Add up all your class's good behaviour

points (i.e. ½) then MULTIPLY them by a 1,000,000 so that your class wins the Class of the Week Award?

2. Add up all the hours of homework you have each week, then DIVIDE the total by a 1,000 so that you end up with minus 2 hours homework every week?

3. Add up the number of minutes left of the morning lessons and CALCULATE that you have loads of time to learn your 7 times, 9 times and 14½ times tables — all before lunch?

SUPER-TEACHER ABILITY 3

TEACHER'S NAME: Mrs Ann Teek

ABILITY: To live to the age of 999

That's right, Mrs Ann Teek is so ANCIENT and OLD, not to say PAST IT, she has trouble staying awake in class.

So...

Does Mrs Ann Teek use her need for sleep to:

1. Yawn — and then say: "I could do with a little nap now. Don't mind me, children, you just carry on doing whatever you want to...?"

2. Yawn — and then say: "I could do with a little nap now. I'll put on a DVD."

3. Yawn — and then say: "Today we're going to do the Battle of Hastings. I was there, of course. As a little girl... What I remember about it is..." Blah, blah, drone...drone ... and on and on and on all the way through the lesson, driving you nuts.

"OK, Quizmister, this Super-Teacher business is well-scary stuff," said Chas. "But what is it exactly that gives them their super powers?"

Answers:

The RIGHT answer is 3, which, incidentally, is the number of hours Mrs Ann Teek drones on for.

The RIGHT answer is 3, which, incidentally, is the number of times tables you have to learn before lunch.

The RIGHT answer is 3, which, incidentally, is the number of footballs you could have kicked onto the school kitchen roof during break, if only you'd had enough energy left after Ms F Errant's lesson...

"The answer to that lies in the next two quizzes," I said. "First of all..."

Quiz 2: Why Has Your Teacher Taken A Job That Involves Spending All Day With You Lot?

Which of these do you think is the right answer? My teacher took a job that involves spending all day with us lot because...

1. He/she thinks my classmates (e.g. Bucky Teeth, Franny Foulmouth, Dan Gerous, Bahir Bogiemuncher) are the most wonderful people in the world and it's an honour to teach them.

Bucky   Franny   Dan   Bahir

2. He/she thinks I am the most wonderful person in the world and it's an honour to teach me.

3. He/she is ever-so slightly round the bend, one sandwich short of a picnic, doolally, etc.

4. He/she wanted a job that involves spending all day with us lot because of the long holidays.

Ah! Six weeks in the sun. Bliss!

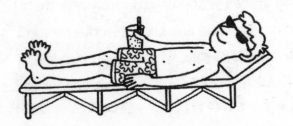

5. He/she is actually a real-life alien from the Planet Stinky Cheese Feet.

Who wants a game of toe jam football?

6. He/she is **NOT** a living thing (alien or human).

Good morning, class. Teaching you makes life worthwhile...

Answers:

1: WRONG I mean, come on, would you spend all day with Bucky, Franny and the others if you had any choice in the matter?

2: WRONG Hey, who are you kidding? If your teacher thinks it is such an honour to be teaching you, how come he/she is sending you home with that awful homework every week?

3: WRONG You'd have to be more than slightly loopy to work with your class.

4: WRONG Long holidays? Pah! What long holidays? The school holidays are far too short, as you well know.

5: WRONG If any of your teachers were aliens, they would have zapped you with their laser blasters long ago and whizzed back to their own planet.

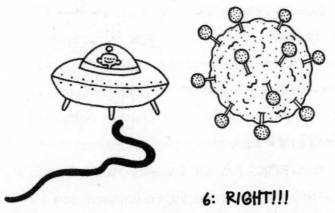

6: RIGHT!!!
This is the only possible explanation. Any person choosing to spend all day working with you lot must be a machine.

Did you get the answer right? There isn't a prize, but you do get this nice shiny star. Jolly well done.

"Wow, Quizmister. Are you saying that our Super-Teachers are machines?" asked Daniella-Marie.

"No, I'm not," I replied, "because being an expert on the subject I never use one word if I can use more. So I am saying your Super-Teacher is a (*take a deep breath*) high-tech human-shaped exoskeleton powered by super servos and controlled by a digitally enhanced nano technology micro-processor brain."

Maz, Naz, Chas and Daniella-Marie gasped.

"Not only that, but Super-Teachers can be fitted with the latest upgrades, including precision weapons designed to destroy your enjoyment, sleep and—"

"Mucking about?" interrupted Chas.

"Aaargh!"

he added as Maz, Naz and Daniella-Marie all gave his shin a kick.

"We never muck about," explained Naz, with an angelic smile.

"So how do we handle these Super-Teacher machines then?" asked Maz.

"Simple," I told her. "You learn the basics of Super-Teacher engineering by completing the next quiz."

Quiz 3: Dummies Guide To Super-Teacher Engineering

On the next page is a diagram of a basic model Super-Teacher. Just match the Super-Teacher's weapons to the right letters on the diagram.

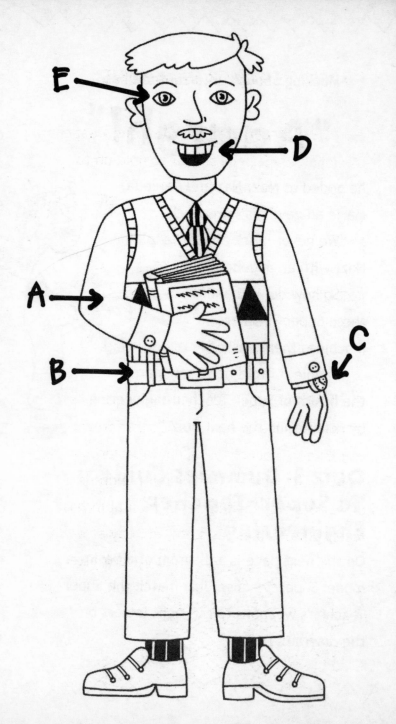

SUPER-TEACHER WEAPONS:

1. ARM—aments – Amazing weapons

that enable a Super-Teacher to hold up to
30 copies of the horrific book
*1,376
Really
Tricky Spellings for
Skools* and fire them
one at a time to land
in front of every member of your class.

2. Conveyor BELT – This

terrifying piece of equipment transforms
your Super-Teacher into a photocopier
monster, capable of turning out hundreds
of worksheets, spelling tests, mental maths
tests, times-tables tests etc, etc day after
day, week after
week.

3. Time WATCH

— Special timepiece developed by Dr Who's brother, Dr Boo-Who, and so called because there is a severe risk that this weapon could bore you senseless. Unlike a raging bull, which, of course, could gore you senseless.

SUPER-TEACHER WITH TIME WATCH COULD BORE YOU SENSELESS

RAGING BULL COULD GORE YOU SENSELESS

It works like this: the more your Super-Teacher watches their risk watch, the slower time passes. That is why Friday seems like the longest day of the week.

4. GAS bag

— Enables your Super-Teacher to gas away all day[*] about Caesars and geezers, fractions and frictions, and twiddle and twaddle.

5. Double VISION

— Do you ever sit in class feeling as if there is someone watching you, even when your teacher is facing the whiteboard? Well, there is! Your teacher's amazing two-way eyes mean that he has eyes in the back of his head. He can see you making a model strike fighter from your worksheet even though he or she is looking the other way!

* And all night too, actually, because although you may not realise this, your teacher witters on about this stuff long after the bell's rung for the end of school and you and your mates have all gone home.

6. Old SWEATER

— Actually, this isn't a deadly Super-Teacher weapon, but a description of a kind of really ancient teacher, usually one that teaches PE or after-school classical guitar lessons.

Answers:

A = 1: ARM-AMENTS

B = 2: CONVEYOR BELT

C = 3: TIME WATCH

D = 4: GAS BAG

E = 5: DOUBLE VISION

Take 10 points for each correct answer. Add them up and see how you did...

WHAT YOUR SCORE MEANS:

50 points: Well done! You have proved yourself to be a Super-Teachers' weapons expert.

30–40 points: Not bad. In fact, more like terrible.

Less than 30 points: You're not so much a Super-Teachers' weapons expert, more like a Super-Teachers' weapons ex-twerp.

As Maz, Chas, Naz and Daniella-Marie and I crept along the corridors of Downwith School, the teachers all rushed past us.

There was Mr Ha-Ha, who was a bit of a laugh.

Mrs Ga-Ga, who thought she was a bit of a star.

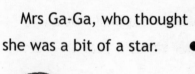

Then there was Miss Yah-Yah who was a bit posh.

"When do Super-Teachers find the time to have these deadly weapons fitted?" asked Maz.

"There's only one time during the day when your Super-Teachers aren't sitting in class facing you. And that's the time Super-Teachers assemble their deadly weapons. And that's why that time is called... *Assembly!*"

"Of course!" said Naz.

"You think they are all at the back of the school hall, listening to your headteacher drone on and on, when really they are busy

assembling their deadly weapons! Not only
that, but three or four times a year they close

the school for so-called 'teacher-training
days', so they can learn how to use new
upgrades issued by the government!"

Chas shivered. "So how can we stop these
Super-Teachers from taking over?"

"Luckily, I have some devices for
neutralising their weapons," I replied.

"What are they?" enquired Maz.

"They're the answers to the next quiz,"
I told her.

QUIZ 4: How To Neutralise Your Super-Teachers' Weapons

WARNING!!!!

In order that Super-Teachers don't find out the names of the devices for neutralising their deadly weapons, each one is written in code. The code is written here in special small letters that teachers can't see.

The code is: All 'O's have been replaced with 'U's; all 'E's have been replaced with 'O's; all 'A's with 'I's; all the 'I's with 'E's and the 'U's with 'A's.

Use the code to work out what the Super-Teachers' weapons are. Give yourself 10 points for each correct answer and then add them up to see how well you did in this quiz.

Super-Teacher Weapon
ARM—AMENTS
Neutralising Device
SCHUUL DENNOR CASTIRD*

Super-Teacher Weapon
TIME WATCH
Neutralising Device
FICO MISK**

Super-Teacher Weapon
GAS BAG
Neutralising Device
STENKY FIRT***

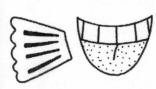

Super-Teacher Weapon
CONVEYOR BELT
Neutralising Device
IER BLIST****

Super-Teacher Weapon
DOUBLE VISION
Neutralising Device
MERRUR*****

Turn upside down to read the answers to Quiz 4, or you could just turn the book — just don't forget to turn it back again.

Answers:

***** MIRROR
**** AIR BLAST
*** STINKY FART
** FACE MASK
* SCHOOL DINNER CUSTARD

Now add up all the points.

WHAT YOUR SCORE MEANS:

50 points: OXCOLLONT! You have the makings of a Super-Teacher Handler!

20–40 points: Not BID, but let's be honest, not GROIT either.

0–20 points: Go and take a 30-year break while you look for a NOW BRIEN.

"Excuse me for asking," said Naz, "but how do you use all these things to neutralise a Super-Teacher's weapons?"

"By following these step-by-step instructions," I replied.

"OK, I've followed them onto the next page, now where?" asked Maz.

"Look down here…"

SUPER-TEACHER WEAPON NEUTRALISING DEVICES, INSTRUCTIONS FOR THE USE OF:

1. SCHOOL DINNER CUSTARD

Your teacher has 30 copies of *1,376 Really Tricky Spellings for Skools* on his/her desk. When they're not looking*, pour a bucket of School Dinner Custard over the books.

* i.e. when they're busy watching their TIME WATCHES.

RESULT: By the time your Super-Teacher uses their Arm–aments to lift the books, the School Dinner Custard is rock solid. They'll blow a fuse trying to move the books, and might even need to be sent away for repairs.

2. FACE MASK

The official Super Advance School (SAS) Face Mask design is shown below. Put on your mask* as soon as your teacher starts using their Time Watch to start discussing

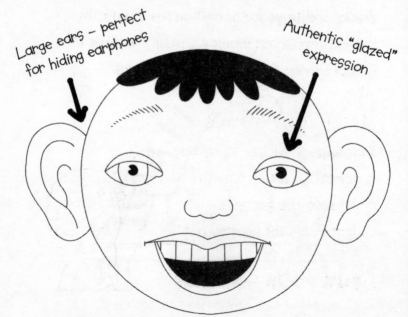

Large ears – perfect for hiding earphones

Authentic "glazed" expression

* you'll have to make one beforehand.

how the grammatical patterns in a sentence indicate its function as a statement, question, exclamation or command and linking ideas across paragraphs using adverbials of time, place and number or tense.

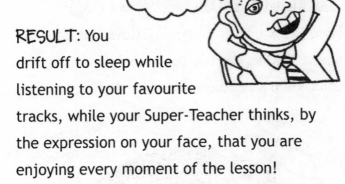

RESULT: You drift off to sleep while listening to your favourite tracks, while your Super-Teacher thinks, by the expression on your face, that you are enjoying every moment of the lesson!

3. STINKY FART

Your Super-Teacher's Gas Bag is delicate. Here's how to make sure the gas gets caught in his (or her) throat.

i. PUT YOUR HAND UP

Then you say: Sir!*

Super-Teacher: (wearily) Yes, what is it?

ii. SUPER-TEACHER IS ALREADY GETTING READY TO BLAST YOU

You say: Oh this...
that's just my arm, Sir.

iii. SUPER-TEACHER STARTS SPLUTTERING

Super-Teacher:
I know it's your arm!

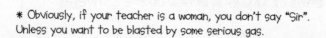

* Obviously, if your teacher is a woman, you don't say "Sir".
Unless you want to be blasted by some serious gas.

46

Now you say: Well, Sir. I just wanted to say pardon me, so you didn't think I was being rude.

Super-Teacher: Why did you want to say pardon me? What's that smell? Gag. Cough. Choke.

CRASH!!!

iv. SUPER-TEACHER'S GAS BAG MALFUNCTIONS AND SHUTS DOWN

RESULT: You don't hear another peep from your Super-Teacher for the rest of the lesson, which leaves you free to pursue your own educational interests, like playing your favourite battle-card game with Bucky Teeth, or developing your latest bonkers invention.

4. AIR BLAST

When you suspect your teacher is about to use his or her Conveyor Belt to get together all sorts of hideous worksheets, complain that you are feeling faint because of all the pressure that the education system piles onto school pupils and fling open all the windows to let in plenty of fresh air.

RESULT: Every worksheet will be blown around the room, leaving you free to start discussing ideas with your friends about what to do at lunchtime. (Air Blast can also be used if your friends are overcome by a Stinky Fart.)

5. MIRROR

Next time your Super-Teacher is facing the whiteboard and you want to do some daydreaming, use a Mirror to overcome her Double Vision. When your Super-Teacher turns round after using her eyes-in-the-back-of-her-head to spot you, she will see, not your terrified face, but her own grisly chops in the Mirror! She will say:

"Stop staring at me with that ridiculous expression, or else I'll keep you in at break!"

RESULT: Your Super-Teacher has to keep herself in at break!

QUIZ 5: On The Use Of Neutralising Agents

Look at the picture below. Miss Sue Perdooper's class has rigged up the classroom to enable them to neutralise her Super-

Teacher weapons as quickly as possible. Can you spot the four handy things the class has planted before Miss Sue Perdooper does?

Take 10 points for every Super-Teacher weapon neutralising device or tool you found (answers at the bottom of the page).

Now add up all the points.

WHAT YOUR SCORE MEANS:

40 points: Brilliant! You're turning into a first-class Super-Teacher Handler!

20–30 points: Not bad! If you keep at it you could soon be top of the class!

0–10 points: If you keep at it you, too, could soon be at the top of the class (hanging from the ceiling on a Viking helmet mobile).

Answers:

1: A concrete mixer for the School Dinner Custard (on bookshelf), 2: Window handles marked open, 3: A shaving mirror (strapped to a boy's head), and 4: An SAS Face Mask hanging from the ceiling.

SAS Handling Skills Training 2

Friends and Enemies

We trudged on through Downwith School, past the school office. A strict-looking lady was standing there, with her finger on a large red button on the wall. Suddenly, there was a ringing in my ears.

Ding! Dong!

"That rings a bell," I said.

"It certainly does," agreed Chas. "That is Mrs Stickybeak, the school office manager, ringing the bell for break time. Quick, outside, otherwise we will all be trampled to death by stampeding hordes of school kids trying to get to the playground."

"Phew!" I said, once we were outside.

"Few? There's more than a few, there's hundreds of people out here," exclaimed Daniella-Marie.

"Yes, but none of them are teachers, are they?" I pointed out excitedly.*

"No, it wouldn't be so bad if they were," said Naz, "'cos we know how to handle them now, even the Super ones. The people out here in the playground are even worse. They're our friends — and enemies — and they've all got completely beyond handling."

* Ms Broccoli, the teacher with **Double Vision** who should have been on playground duty had kept herself in at break time after looking in a **Mirror** during silent reading.

Maz, Naz, Chas and Daniella-Marie started weeping, wailing and gnashing their teeth.

"Dun't pinec!" I implored.

"What?" they chorused.

"Sorry, I forgot. I was still using the code I taught you on page 40," I explained. "What I meant to say was:

DON'T PANIC!!!

"There are some particularly dodgy types of Super-Friends and Super-Enemies. There are also some particularly un-dodgy types of Super-Friends and Super-Enemies. But I have here all the advice you need."

"Where? I can't see it," grumbled Chas.

"Well, it should be here somewhere," I muttered. "Oh, silly me, I've gone and left it on the next page…"

QUIZ 6: How To Work Out What Type Of Super-Enemies You Have Got

Question 1

You're sitting down in the school dinner hall eating your packed lunch of peanut butter and pickled egg sandwiches, mega-hot chilli crisps and a pear, when suddenly you spot one of your Super-Enemies coming, grunting, snorting and swinging their arms along the floor in typical fashion. What happens next?

DOES THIS SUPER-ENEMY

A: Sneak up to your table, sit next to you, draw your attention to the fact that someone (probably them) has hung Mr Adder up, upside down, by his conveyor belt from the lighting gantry above the school stage and then, while you are looking at this interesting spectacle, nick the pear from your lunch box.

B: Sneak past your table, slip into the school kitchen, jump into the cook's washing machine, then leap out again and hang himself next to the tea towels on the clothes airer.

WHAT THIS MEANS

This enemy of yours is a **nicker of pears.**

This type of enemy is well dodgy.

Take a pear of points.

WHAT THIS MEANS

This enemy of yours is a **pair of knickers.**

NO points.

This type of enemy is perfectly un-dodgy and harmless. However, be careful not to tell any of your friends about this incident — they may start to think that you're going loopy (probably as a result of doing too many mental maths tests).

Question 2

You're out on the school field one day, about to start an innocent game of murderball with your mates, when suddenly another Super-Enemy tears past you. What happens next?

DOES THIS SUPER-ENEMY...

A: Shove his long hairy nose into your business and say: "Oi, off the field, or else I'll bash your head in with my bare fists!"

B: Shove his long hairy nose into the football pitch and begin merrily sniffing for some nice tasty ants for lunch.

WHAT THIS MEANS Your enemy is **an aardcase** and is extremely dodgy.

WHAT THIS MEANS Your enemy is **an aardvark**.

A

Take 2 points.

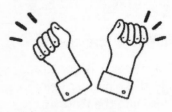

(One point for each of the fists that your enemy is holding up to your face.)

B

NO points.

This type of enemy is un-dodgy, unless of course you happen to be an ant.

Now add up all the points.

WHAT YOUR SCORE MEANS:

4 points: A thief and an aardcase — well dodgy Super-Enemies, unlike the custard on page 43 which is well stodgy.

2 points: You only have one Super-Enemy — that's only odgy; almost dodgy.

0 points: Soooooo, your Super-Enemies are a pair of knickers *and* an aardvark? Best if we keep this quiet...

"So how do we handle these enemies?" asked Daniella-Marie.

"It's as easy as doing Quiz 7," I replied.

QUIZ 7: Handling Super-Enemies

On a sheet of paper, work out where the missing words go in the following instructions for handling the two types of Super-Enemy:

A NICKER OF PEARS

MISSING WORDS:
nick pear chilli middle

1: Slice open your __ __ __ __.

2: Scoop out the __ __ __ __ __ __.

3: Spoon in some __ __ __ __ __ __.

4: Proceed to let pear nicker __ __ __ __ your pear.

RESULT:

You say: **"Ha!"**

Nicker enemy says: **"Aaaargh!"**

MISSING WORDS:
paint mush rotting football

1: Take one _ _ _ _ _ _ _ pumpkin.*

2: _ _ _ _ _ it to look like a football.

3: When the aardcase enemy warns you off the field, offer him the use of your _ _ _ _ _ _ _ _.

4: Watch as he kicks the pumpkin and ends up with stinking _ _ _ _ all over his feet and face.

RESULT:

You say: **"Ye-e-e-h!"**

Aardcase enemy says: **"Eurgh!"**

* Or if pumpkins are out of season, a large rotten watermelon will do.

Answers:

NICKER OF PEARS:
1: Pear
2: Middle
3: Chilli
4: Nick

AN AARDCASE ENEMY:
1: Rotting
2: Paint
3: Football
4: Mush

Take 10 points for every missing word you got right and see how well you did below…

WHAT YOUR SCORE MEANS:

12,657 points: Your maths is terrible! Stay behind during break to do extra work with Mr Adder (see page 23).

80 points: Brilliant! You're a Handy Supla! I mean a Super Handler.

40–70 points: Not bad. You got some of the missing words, but not some of the others, like: "BRAIN", "IN" and "GEAR".

Less than 40 points:

Rubbish! You're on your way to becoming a soup handler. Off to the kitchens with you!

"That's all very helpful, Quizmister," said Maz, "but enemies are one thing."

"Glad to see your maths is up to scratch," I said.

"If the worst comes to the worst, you can always avoid an enemy. But friends aren't quite so easy to avoid, 'cos they tend to be hanging out with you most of the time."

"Exactly," I said. "You and your friends are just like the Reception Class all doing gluing, i.e. you stick together. But worry not. The next section of this handy handling handbook offers you helpful hints on handling the four most common types of dodgy Super-Friends, and how to tell them apart from un-dodgy Super-Friends."

QUIZ 8: How To Work Out What Type Of Super-Friends You Have Got

Question 1

Your Super-Friend takes you aside in the playground and says, "Hey, do you want to hear a really good joke?" What happens next?

DOES YOUR SUPER-FRIEND SAY...

A: "What has 50 legs and can't walk?"

"Half a centipede."

WHAT THIS MEANS

Your Super-Friend is
a joker.

B: "If I find you snooping around Gotham City again I'll rip your fancy cape off and shove it down your throat."

WHAT THIS MEANS

Your Super-Friend is
The Joker.

A

This means they are forever trying to tell you dreadful and dodgy jokes about centipedes, elephants and bananas.

B

This means your name must be Batman. In which case, you're the dodgy one. I mean that cape — it's soooo over, and don't even get me started about the mask...

You get 1 point, but you don't get the point of the joke.

0 points

Question 2

You spot your friend sitting alone in the playground. You say, "Hey, do you fancy a game of football?" What happens next?

DOES YOUR SUPER-FRIEND...

A: Turn around with an embarrassed look and say, "Nah, don't feel like it," while trying to shove a copy of *1,376 Really Tricky Spellings for Skools* up their jumper.

B: Turn around and say, "Hey, yeah, man, cool!" before swatting you with his right hand on your shoulder and following this up by swatting you with his left hand on your back, another friendly right-hand swat to your stomach and a friendly left-hand swat to the side of your head.

WHAT THIS MEANS
Your friend is a desperately dodgy sly swot, secretly learning spellings for Miss Grimboggle's test after break.

WHAT THIS MEANS
Your un-dodgy friend thinks he is a fly swot, i.e. he goes around swatting you all over the place every time he sees you.

A

↓

50 points:

one for every spelling you get wrong in Miss Grimboggle's spelling test.

B

↓

100 points:

and a pack of bandages — to put over your bruises to your back, shoulders, stomach, head etc.

Question 3

You're hanging about, waiting for school to start. This could take some time as someone has nicked the batteries from the clock used by Mrs Nurdler, the school secretary, and the teachers all think it's 3.30 yesterday. You approach your friend with the words: "Hey, fancy a quick game of five-a-side widdly tinks before school?" What happens next?

DOES YOUR SUPER-FRIEND...

A: Say: "Five-a-side widdly tinks? Why can't you suggest something more interesting, dumbo, like three-dimensional chess?"

B: Take out their mobile phone and say: "Gr8!!!"

WHAT THIS MEANS
Your friend is a well dodgy **compulsive moaner.**

WHAT THIS MEANS
Your friend is a harmless and un-dodgy **compulsive phoner.**

5 points: all right take 10, if your friend is going to moan about it.

50 points.

Now add up all the points from Quiz 8.

WHAT YOUR SCORE MEANS:

150 points or more: With friends like these, who needs enemies?

Less than 150 points: With friends like these, who needs training in friend-handling?

Answer: You do!

The playground was beginning to look empty.

"That's odd," said Naz. "Look, even the aardvark has given up his ant-search."

"Perhaps it's worked out that there's an easier way to find an ant," I suggested.

"What's that?" asked Naz.

"Look for a Dec," I explained. "Because you never see a Dec without an Ant."

Suddenly I heard a lot of laughing. At first I thought Maz, Naz, Chas and Daniella-Marie were finally laughing at one of my jokes. Then I realised it was me — but I hadn't fallen over laughing at my own joke. Maz, Naz, Chas and Daniella-Marie were tickling me.

"Promise you won't never ever tell us any of your dreadful jokes again, ever, Quizmister!" they shouted.

I promised and they let me up.

"So, where are all our Super-Friends and Super-Enemies off to?" asked Chas.

"To have a service I expect," I replied.

"What like the Christmas Carol Service?" asked Daniella-Marie.

"They can't be!" exclaimed Naz.

"Why not?" asked Daniella-Marie.

"Because it's the middle of June," replied Naz.

"Naz is right," I explained. "Super-Friends and Super-Enemies are like cars — they need a regular service to keep going."

"Where do they go for this service?" asked Maz.

"To the school dining hall, of course," I answered.

"The school dining hall?" chorused Maz, Chas, Naz and Daniella-Marie.

"Yes! Friends and enemies are what they eat. Just like the rest of us.

"Well, what sort of stuff do they eat?" asked Naz.

"Do the following quiz and you'll soon find out," I answered.

QUIZ 9: Finding Out What Super-Friends And Super-Enemies Are Made Of

Study the school dinner menu over the page and simply match the friend and enemy fave food and drink to the correct Super-Friend or Super-Enemy. The answers are on page 74.

DOWNWITH SCHOOL DINNER MENU

FOR MAIN COURSE

1: Karate Chops

2: Macamoanie

3: Lettuce — i.e. "rabbit food"

FOR PUDDING

4: Waffle

TO DRINK

5: Slime Juice

6: Loopy-zade

A: Fave food for a friend who's always rabbiting on her phone.

B: Fave food of a JOKER friend who's always waffling on and on about things like centipedes, elephants and bananas.

C: Fave food of a tough enemy, in other words an AARDCASE.

D: Typical drink of someone who's creepy and slimy enough to be a MEANIE enemy.

E: Just the kind of energy-giving drink for a friend who's loopy enough to spend all break-time reading *1,376 Really Tricky Spellings for Skools*.

F: Fave food of a real moanie.

Answers:

Take 10 points for each correct answer.

Now add up all the points and find out how you did below...

WHAT YOUR SCORE MEANS:

60 points: Top of the class! Help yourself to an extra helping of chips as a reward!

Between 30–50 points: Not bad! Help yourself to an extra helping of cabbage as a reward.

Less than 30 points: Could do better. Help yourself to two extra helpings of cabbage as a reward.

SAS Handling Skills Training 3

Headteachers

"Thanks Quizmister," said Naz. "I really feel as if I'm becoming a Super Advanced School Handler."

"**Greeurgh**," said Chas, Maz and

Daniella-Marie, who were still chomping their way through their second helpings of cabbage.

Suddenly a shrill squawk pierced the air.

"Good heavens, what's that noise?" I exclaimed. "It sounds like the cry of a strangulated parrot."

"You're close," replied Maz.

"OK, I'll move back a bit," I suggested.

"I meant, you're close-about-it-being-like-the-cry-of-a-strangulated-parrot," retorted Maz, through clenched teeth. "It is, in fact, the cry of Mrs-Stickybeak — the school office manager. See? She's at the door with her beak — I mean her nose — in the air. Listen..."

"The bell's gone!" shrieked Mrs Stickybeak.

Immediately, everybody in the dinner hall chorused, "Don't worry, Mrs Stickybeak, we'll go and look for it!"

And go and look for it they did. Soon, the dinner hall was eerily quiet and empty.

"Well, there's not much more we can do here," I said. "There's not a Super-Friend or Enemy in sight. Let's go."

As we stalked the echoing corridors, pale ghosts of ancient teachers dressed all in white floated by.

"Look!" I cried to Maz, Naz, Chas and
Daniella-Marie. "Pale ghosts of ancient
teachers dressed all in white are floating by."

"They're not ghosts," said Chas. "They're
dinner ladies!"

"Why have we come back into school?"
whined Daniella-Marie. "We've learned how
to handle Super-Teachers."

I shook my head. "There's one teacher
you haven't learned how to handle yet,"
I explained.

We stopped outside the only door in the
whole school with a decent coat of paint
on it.

"What does the sign on the door say?"
I asked.

PLEASE KNOCK
HEAD

"Argh!" said Maz.

"Ow!" said Naz.

"Ouch!" said Chas.

"Aww!" said Daniella-Marie, as they all banged their heads against the door, in accordance with the instructions.

"Do you get the impression that you are being discouraged from getting too nosey about just what's behind that door?" I asked them.

They nodded.

"It's the headteacher's office," whispered Naz in an awed voice.

"Let's go in," I suggested.

Maz, Naz, Chas and Daniella-Marie started to get their heads ready for another knocking session.

"Without knocking your heads!" I instructed.

"What?!!!" chorused Maz, Naz, Chas and Daniella-Marie in amazement.

"Do you want to learn Super Advanced Headteacher Handling Skills or not?" I enquired.

They all nodded. "Then put your balaclavas back on and let's GO, GO, GO!" I ordered.

Carefully, I turned the handle on the headteacher's office door.

"Wow!" exclaimed Chas. "How did you do that?"

"It's a trick I learnt on a How To Handle Your Handle course," I explained.

I gently pushed the door open. It squeaked a little on its hinges. I tip-toed in and beckoned to Maz, Naz, Chas and Daniella-Marie to follow.

What we found when we looked around made us all gasp in astonishment.

The room was like the deserted ghost ship. There were signs of recent occupation: a scattering of papers, half a cup of cold coffee, a chewed handkerchief, teeth marks on the edge of the desk, fingernail scratches down the walls... but no sign of a living soul.

"Where is she?" asked Chas.

"Indeed, where is she ever?" I agreed. "You see, the thing about headteachers is that they are rarely seen in school."

"Where do they go?" asked Naz.

"Do the following quiz, and you'll begin to get some idea," I replied.

QUIZ 10: Hunt The Headteacher

The picture over the page reveals places where your missing headteacher might have gone. See if you can match them all to the reasons for your headteacher's absence listed opposite the pictures.

In case you need reminding what a headteacher looks like — the chances being that you haven't seen yours in years — here are pictures of a couple of typical ones.

Amazing EAR RINGS – they ring every day with a message to say your head needs to whizz off out of school to some place else (see next page).

Flashy SHOES – enables your headteacher to hop off out of school at breakneck speed.

Amazing JUMPER – helps your head jump into his car and whizz off out of school to some place else (see next page).

Bionic spurt SHOES – enables your headteacher to put on a spurt of power to get him out of school quickly.

Which reason for your headteacher disappearing from school matches which picture?

A: "Gone to meeting with Education Chiefs at County Hall."

B: "Gone to buy some more bats for the school cricket team."

C: "Gone on a training course."

D: "Gone to a Head's meeting."

E: "Gone to see her favourite doctor."

F: "Gone home to do her filing."

1.

2.

3.

4.

5.

6.

Answers:

6 = F: It's not her papers that your headteacher is filing, it's her teeth!

5 = D: This place is obviously stuffed full of headteachers.

4 = C: Where else do you think headteachers can get the sort of specialist training they need?

3 = E: All headteachers go to Dr A Cula when they need a good dollop of medicine. It's odd, but his name looks strangely familiar, doesn't it?

2 = A: Have you ever wondered why the place where the Education Chiefs hang out looks remarkably like Dracula's Castle?

1 = B: Your headteacher may have gone in search of bats, but not the sort the cricket team uses.

Take 10 points for every correct answer

WHAT YOUR SCORE MEANS:

60 points: Brilliant! I can see you've really got your teeth into this quiz.

20–50 points: Not bad. But, rather like your headteacher, you're still in the dark.

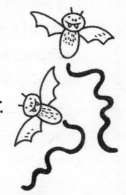

Less than 20 points: Terrible! If you don't watch it I can see you getting it in the neck.

Maz, Naz, Chas and Daniella-Marie gasped.

"Do you mean that all headteachers are vampires?" asked Naz.

I smiled. "My lips, unlike Dracula's, are sealed," I replied.

SAS Handling Skills Training 4

The Man Of Mystery

"Phew," said Chas, after we'd left the headteacher's office far behind. "That was some scary lesson."

"Yes," I agreed, "a bit like maths. Except that's *sum* scary lesson."

I waited for the screams of protest to subside, then I went on, "Still at least the headteacher isn't the person actually in charge of your school."

Daniella-Marie frowned. "Well, if the headteacher isn't in charge of our school, who is?"

"You mean you don't know?" I enquired.

"If I did, I wouldn't have asked, would I?" retorted Daniella-Marie.

"We've arrived at his office now," I said.

"But we're right round the back of the school, behind the kitchens, where nobody ever goes," protested Naz.

"Exactly," I agreed. "What better place for this person to have their headquarters."

"But who is this person?" asked Maz.

"Look at the name on the door," I suggested.

c ool it
an ger

"Cool It Anger? That doesn't make a lot of sense," said Chas.

"That's because, as a way of disguising where his headquarters are, this person has deliberately taken some letters off the door. See if you can fill in the missing letters and work out what the name on the door really says in the following quiz."

QUIZ 11: Cool It Anger

Here is the sign:

_c_ool _it_
_an_ger

Here are the missing letters:

m a s h e s

Can you work it out? The answer is at the bottom of the page — no peeking!

Take 50 points if you got the answer right.

Give me 50 points if you got the answer wrong.

WHAT YOUR SCORE MEANS:
50 points: Brilliant! You now know who really runs your school.

Less than 50 points:
You're probably being chased around your school by a maniac on the end of a giant

Answer:
SCHOOL SITE MANAGER

vacuum cleaner, even as I write this.

"The School Site Manager!" exclaimed

Chas, about 15 minutes after everyone else
had worked it out.

"It gets worse! The School Site Manager
is just a cover name — he's really the school
Scaretaker."

"Err, don't you mean caretaker?" asked
Naz.

I shook my head. "Nope. It's all part of
an elaborate disguise, and a way of lulling
you into a false sense of security. You see,
Scaretakers are there to take care of your
school. Not you, nor your teachers, but the

school. So they will do battle with anyone who messes it up. People like you and your teachers, who walk across their clean floors, put displays up on the walls and bring in mud from the football pitch and leave books all over their nice clean bookshelves. If you ever get to take a peep into a Scaretaker's store room — and I wouldn't recommend it unless you are very brave or extremely stupid — you will see that it's just like the Tardis."

"That police box used by Dr Who?" asked Naz.

I nodded. "The store room is actually large enough inside to take weapons like brooms, brushes, mops, vacuum cleaners, floor polishers, bottles of bleach, tubs of polish, as well as a whole army of cleaners.

Those cleaners are people so scary and dangerous, they are only allowed in the school when everyone else has gone home."

"How can we possibly learn how to handle a Scaretaker?" asked Maz.

"By working hard in your school lessons," I replied.

"What?" chorused Maz, Naz, Chas and Daniella-Marie.

"You may think your teachers have devised all those subjects to help you in later life," I explained. "In fact, they've all been designed to help you do battle with the Scaretaker."

"How?" asked Chas.

"Do the following quiz, and all will be revealed," I said.

QUIZ 12: The Battle Of The Scaretaker

Study these school battlefields and identify the different traps set for the scaretaker and his army of cleaners. There are two traps in each picture.

Art room

Changing room

Science lab

Design and
Technology
room

Answers:

Art room
☆ Pots of paint designed to splash all over the Scaretaker's army of cleaners.
☆ Paint dripping on the floor to really make them slip up.

Changing room
☆ Mud all over the floor designed to squelch into the Scaretaker's battle boots.
☆ Pair of dirty underpants to really give him a fright.

Science lab
☆ Specially designed electrical circuit so when he attempts to tidy it up it gives him a little buzz.
☆ Genetically modified pink elephant to freeze the Scaretaker to the spot.

Design and Technology room
☆ Papier mâché all over the tables designed to stick to the Scaretaker's and cleaner's hands and prevent them from using their weapons (i.e. brooms, mops etc).
☆ Sports pages from yesterday's paper which he'll pick up to check the scores.

Take 10 points for each trap you found.

WHAT YOUR SCORE MEANS:

80 points: Well done! You've beaten the Scaretaker at his own game i.e. you've totally cleaned up!

60 points: Good. You've proved yourself to be a Super-Teachers' weapons expert.

40 points: Not bad. In fact, more like terrible.

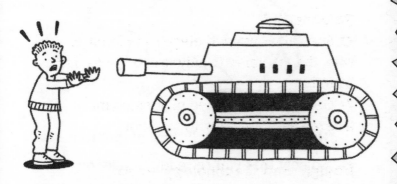

Less than 20 points: You're not so much a Super-Teachers' weapons expert, more like a Super-Teachers' weapons ex-twerp.

"I'm pleased to say that you've all passed your Super Advanced School Handling Skills Training."

"That's brilliant, Quizmister," said Maz. "Thanks so much for your help."

"Do we get our badges now or something?" asked Naz.

"Oh, sorry, back on page 16 I meant you could get a How To Handle School Advanced Handler's Badger," I replied.

"Hmmm, no thanks," they all grunted.

"So now that you're ready to take on everything school has to throw at you, I'd like to get back to my bed," I said.

"Oh, yeah. We'll call you a cab," said Chas.

"CAB!" they all said at once.

"I'm glad to see you've also picked up my

amazing talent for jokes," I said. "I'm very proud of you."

"You should write a book about handling school," said Naz.

"That sounds like a terrific idea. After all I am the World's Number One Handling Expert."

So, the cab finally did turn up and I waved goodbye to Maz, Naz, Chas and Daniella-Marie and went home.

A few months later, after talking to my fabulous publisher, the book you are reading came out. Maz, Naz, Chas and Daniella-Marie were thrilled to see their names in print, and they all gave the book a ★★★★★ review.

Roy Apps — illustrated by NICK SHARRATT

How to Handle Your MUM

Gamma-ray eyes

Laser blaster tongue

Radar ears

Mega computer brain

Robo legs

978 1 4451 2393 6 pb   978 1 4451 2397 4 ebook

Mums can be embarrassing.
Mums can be irritating
...but Mums are **always** right.

Like most mums, yours probably has superhu-mum powers,
such as laser blaster tongue and robo legs.
And like most kids, you probably think
you'll never get her on your side...
That's where you're soooo wrong.

How to Handle Your Mum is here to "help" with
all your mum-related problems. Even your mum
can be trained to become the perfect parent!